I Am Safe

Appreciation for
Nedti-Hand Drawn Doodle Digital Clipart Design
clker.com
wpclipart.com
ISBN-13: 978-1496035097
ISBN-10: 1496035097

Printed in the USA

The people who love me want me to be safe. I want to be safe, too.

Write the names of people who love you.

I wear my seat belt in the car.
Draw a seat belt across the boy's chest.

I wear my helmet when I ride my bike.

Draw a helmet on the girl's head.

I never play with matches, knives or guns.

Circle things that are safe to play with.

If a stranger comes to my door,
I do not open it. I go tell my parents.

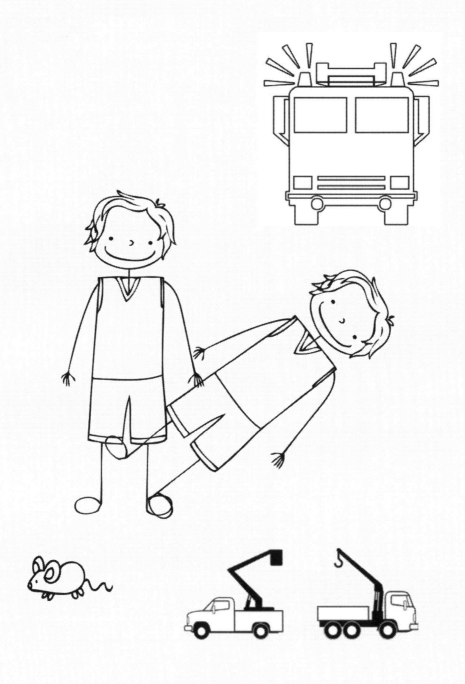

If there is a fire,
I know how to stop, drop and roll.
Can you practice rolling?

Do you know your parents' phone numbers?

I also know that if I am in danger and cannot find my parents or someone I trust, I should call 9-1-1 and ask for help.

The people who love me also want me to be safe from people who do bad things. So I am learning what to do if someone wants to do something bad to me.

If an adult or kid wants me to hurt my
body with smoking or drugs, I will say,
"No way!" and walk away.

Write the words, "No Way!" in the speaking balloon.

If someone I do not know or trust
tells me to get in a car with them,
I will run away as fast as I can, yelling
for help from the first person I see.

If someone steals or does something
bad, and they say if I tell they will do a
bad thing to me, that is a threat. It is
not right. I will still tell someone I trust.

**If anyone tries to give me money
or presents to do something bad
or keep a bad secret, that is a bribe.
I will not take bribes.**
Write what you would say if someone offered you a bribe.

If a stranger sends me a message on a phone or computer, I will show it to my parents.

Draw a phone in the boy's hand.

I respect my body. I am allowed privacy
when I change my clothes.

Draw a privacy curtain or wall between the boy and girl.

I respect other people's bodies.
I will not look at pictures on the TV or computer of people who are changing their clothes or not wearing enough clothes.

Draw a big OFF button on the TV and then push it!

I play with all my clothes on even if I am
playing doctor. No one is allowed to remove
my clothes without my permission.

I know about good touch.
I like to give hugs and high-fives
to people I love and trust.
Can you draw arms on the people to hug or give a high-five?

I also know about bad touch.
If someone tries to touch a private part of
my body, I will yell, "Stop that right now!"
I will get away from that person right
away and go tell someone I trust.
Draw the boy's hands out in a STOP motion.

Someday I might be in a room by myself with only one adult. If I am uncomfortable, I will leave that room right away.
Draw an EXIT door for the girl.

I do not have to obey an adult who
does bad things. If anyone tries to do a
bad thing to me, I will scream and kick
and try my best to get away.

Circle the animals that would be dangerous.
How can you tell if a person is dangerous?

I know that if someone does a
bad thing to me, it is not my fault. No
matter what they say, I did not do wrong
and should not keep it a secret.

Write the names of people you would tell
if something bad happened to you.

If someone tells me I am stupid or ugly
or do not matter, I will not believe them.
I know I am special. I will not let
anyone hurt my heart or my body.

What are some things about you that are special?

The world has lots and lots of
good people in it. I will talk to the people
I love and trust about what is happening
to me and how I feel.

With their help, I will make the choices
that help keep me safe.

MY LIST

THINGS THAT ARE SPECIAL ABOUT ME:

1. _____

2. _____

3. _____

PEOPLE WHO LOVE ME AND WANT ME TO BE SAFE:

1. _____

2. _____

3. _____

PEOPLE I TRUST WHO I CAN ASK FOR HELP:

1. _____

2. _____

3. _____

FIND MORE RESOURCES AT
www.kimberlyrae.com

Made in the USA
San Bernardino, CA
03 July 2016